52

TOTALLY UNIQUE
THEME PARTIES

by Patty Sachs

52 TOTALLY UNIQUE THEME PARTIES

by Patty Sachs

Copyright © 1993 Patty Sachs

CELEBRATION CREATIONS
7817 - 67th Avenue North
Minneapolis, MN 55428

Cover art by Leisa Luis
Text layout by Laser Set of Minnetonka
Page design and creative collaboration by Maridee Ennis

First Printing, this edition, October, 1993
ISBN 0-9616680-3-2

52
TOTALLY UNIQUE THEME PARTIES

The party plans in this little book are scant descriptions of unique theme concepts. The book has been written in a "random • thought • style" which, though not literary, will give you a helpful jump-start on your creative brainstorming.

The party categories are Invitations, Decor, Dress, Activities, Prizes/Favors, Refreshments and special details. With a little of your own research, withdrawals from the idea banks of people in your midst, blended with your brilliant thoughts, you'll have theme power to spare.

To enhance the mini-plans in this book you can include d.j. or live music for listening and dancing, photographers, videographers, as well as the suggested specialty party entertainment.

While designing and planning your theme it is desirable to develop even the smallest details to assure your party's success. There's "almost" no such thing as too cute or too gimmicky. Caution: If you would like your event plan to include twelve clever theme activities or details, plan fifteen because two or three will fizzle—no fault of yours.

Setting the Theme

If you are deciding upon a theme for a party that is in honor of a person(s), the theme will sometimes be very obvious. Themes are usually based on occupations, hobbies, talents, interests, characteristics, personalities or idiosyncrasies. For business purposes, themes are usually more strait-laced and sophisticated. But for private celebrations, the stops are pulled and themes are often hilarious spoofs and sometimes way-out in concept.

Example: A coed wedding shower was planned for a couple that was obsessively neat and organized. The theme was just that—"A Tribute to Two Neat People." The plan included an invitation printed on an index card and sent with a Rolodex card, post-it-note and paper clip; guests were given arrival times minutes apart to avoid any confusion or rush; guests had to line up in alphabetical order for their dinners; all of the gifts were of the organizational variety; immediately after the bride opened the gifts, the groom had to register them on a card and file them neatly in a file box.

Another example: One guest of honor had a reputation for premature party cleanup. He would begin emptying ashtrays and picking up dirty glasses at least two hours before the party was scheduled to end. Close friends and relatives were invited to celebrate his milestone birthday by attending a "Garbage Bag Birthday Bash." Some of the party fun included: invitation written on small garbage bag; guests were instructed to wear garbage bag fashions; buffet table was decorated with all sorts of plastic bag creations; at 10 pm all guests stood, left the room, returned with huge trash bags and began to police the area...a great party that took its theme from a quirky habit.

Once that you have decided to produce a party with a theme, your job will be much easier. The theme is a virtual road map to guide you along the way. First, make a list of every item, person, place, song, book, product, activity or fact that fits even remotely into your theme. Give the list long thought—share it with others. The things you select from that list will be the stops on your journey to a perfect party destination.

Invitations

- Follow post office regulations when addressing envelopes. (See resource section.)

- Address envelopes in ink color matching invitation ink color.

- Use the prettiest stamps available, following your theme, if possible.

- Decorate envelope to match invitation.

- Put names of all guests on envelope, including children.

- Neatly typed is better than poorly written.

- Typed labels are very impersonal; but if absolutely necessary, use fancy lettering and add decoration or trim.

- For family functions, send invitation to children and instruct them to bring their parents. Get ready for a near 100% turnout.

- Make sure that your invitation gives all information that a person would need to be a perfect guest. Include:

  What, where, when and why

  If you are inviting adults only, a gracious way to state this is "Parents night out"

  Dress code

  Gift policy

  What to bring (food, beverage, etc.)

  Meal, if any, that will be served

  Times of special presentations

  Directions to event site

  Map, if necessary

  RSVP number and time to call

- RSVP mail-back card may request: first and last names of all guests, entrée choice (if applicable), special seating needs, whether guest wishes to present a toast or special message during the program or have it given by another.

- Ask for a Yes or No response. By requesting "Regrets Only" you will have no way of knowing if an invitation was not received.

Name Tags and Place Cards

Name tags and place cards are highly recommended for utmost organization and will most likely need to be handmade to match your theme. Guests are complimented and impressed when they arrive to find their name tag and/or place card waiting.

Name tags are desirable at both personal and business related events, especially when guests represent a mix of work or school mates; association and church members; family, friends and neighbors. When wearing clearly printed name tags, your guests will feel secure and comfortable as they socialize with each other.

Name tag tips:

Write names in large block letters in water proof ink.

Do not ever let guests write their own tags.

Establish whether tags are safe for fine fabrics.

Alternatives to adhesive name tags are ribbons, flowers, party buttons, bibs, visors, hats, around the neck hang tags.

Name tag placement is on the right lapel, for ease in reading while shaking another's hand.

If an official greeter helps guests with name tags, they will more readily wear them.

Close quarters? Place name tags on outside of apartment door to greet guests. Arrange in shape of wreath for holidays or in the form of a heart on Valentine's Day, etc.

Example: A Pig Roast party host provided a plastic bib for each guest with his/her name written on it.

To further assure your guests' comfort, use place cards to assign each a reserved seat for dining, thus removing their "where-should-I-sit?" anxiety. Some people go to great trouble to seat guests with others who would be compatible. A stress-reducing idea is to simply number each person's place card or name tag (couples stay together) with a table number and let the cards fall where they may...excuse the pun. This simple plan encourages some interesting blends and spirited conversations.

Place card tips:

Best if beautifully written or printed.

Rather than Mr. & Mrs. use guests first names; i.e., Sally and Jim Smith.

Prepare separate place cards for each child. This small gesture goes a long way in pleasing a youngster.

Alternatives to place cards are tiny gift-wrapped packages (could be candy); party buttons; bags of popcorn; theme items including baseballs, Hawaiian leis, Italian bread sticks, or Chinese fortune cookies.

Example: A delicious place card idea is to tie a small gift card on the stem of a shiny red apple.

Some trimmings suggestions for name tags or place cards following your theme:

Nautical—peppermint Lifesaver

Musical—musical note sticker or charm

Shower—cocktail umbrella

Italian—pasta in novelty shapes

Travel—foreign stamps

Mystery—tiny magnifying glass

Casino—miniature playing cards

Fifties—bubble gum (Bazooka)

Circus—popped popcorn or Crackerjack

Chinese—tiny folding fan

Always arrange name tags and place cards in alphabetical order, either on a table or affixed to an attractively decorated easel board.

Theme Party Details

There are a few party details that work for almost any party, although I have mentioned them in only a few of the plans. The following is a more in-depth description of those components.

Video and Watch: The highly visual parties—those with costumes, elaborate decor and activities worth documenting—are worthy of video taping. These tapes provide sensational entertainment for the guests during the party.

You might video tape the entrance and introduction of all guests then show the results during the party. Another idea is to video tape until the last hour and then show the tape for a nice recap during the nightcaps.

Voice Mail: Every theme design could benefit from a special RSVP voice mail message. When guests call in they listen to a theme-geared message, then leave their response.

This method of collecting responses has a three-fold benefit. First, a lively, musical and humorous message gets the guests in the party mood, which is your goal. Second, it diverts the phone calls coming in to your home or office that might spoil a surprise; and for most busy people, take up a great deal of time. The final benefit is that the calls can be made 24 hours a day, to the guests' convenience.

Most answering bureaus have a one-month service that will cost about $25.00. You will thoroughly enjoy the enthusiastic messages that come in response to your clever greeting.

Instant Photos: It would be a shame to pass up an opportunity to photograph your guests at their most ridiculous or ravishing best. Take instant photos of your guests against a special photo backdrop or prop setting. A frame of cardboard, plastic or wood to match your theme will be a wonderful addition. These photos will be a premium gift and an everlasting memory of your event.

The 52 themes that are featured in this book will be suitable for special events of all description. With a little imagination, you can adapt most of them to your particular reason to celebrate.

CELEBRATIONS OR EVENTS PLANNED WITH THEMES

Anniversary
Baby Shower, Coed
Baby Shower, Ladies Only
Bar/Bat Mitzvah
Birthday
Church or School Event
Class Reunion
Client Appreciation
Club or Association Event
Company Party
Company Picnic
Engagement
Family Reunion
First Birthday
Fund raiser
Going Away/Welcome Home
Graduation
Holiday Party
Retirement
Store Promotion
Wedding
Wedding Shower, Coed
Wedding Shower, Ladies Only

TABLE OF CONTENTS

What Is All the Excitement
about Theme Parties?

Theme parties are exciting! Your party can be elaborate, extravagant, gimmicky, funny, corny, sentimental or sophisticated. A theme (definition: a subject or topic recurring throughout) analogously serves as a "destination" for your event. From the moment the invitation is received until the grand finale, your guests are united in a special "something in common" way.

What Are the Benefits of Using a Theme
When Planning an Event?

A theme is a road map, a take-along list, an itinerary and a menu. Armed with those tools, you will find it easier to succeed. By using a theme, you automatically zero in on a limited amount of choices, making it clear what details your final plan might include.

A.M. AEROBICS

A great theme for a brunch party celebrating either health-nut athletic enthusiasts or wanna-be's. Wake 'em up...and shake 'em up with this energetic, invigorating and entertaining event.

Invitation: Printed and rolled inside a terry wrist or head band...name of the guest of honor, date, etc. embroidered or printed on band. [For real jocks send real jocks! Novelty/gag shops carry them in miniature, to be used for drink glass coasters.]

Dress: In exercise sweats • Dance gear • Comfortable, casual clothing

Activities: Rousing blast of aerobecizing music to greet guests as they enter • Person dressed as a nurse to take vitals • First prize to the best sport • Token calisthenics • A brisk walk around the block • Jazzercize • Ambitious aerobics • Video tape, and for a cool down exercise, watch tape • [For a coed baby shower try some laid back "labor-intensive" breathing exercises.] • A hot exercise video for more sedentary guests...to watch. [Caution: Don't let them over-exert by watching too long...Remember, laughter burns calories too.]

Decor: Health and nutrition posters • Exercise equipment • A marathon banner • Covers of fitness and health magazines • Fresh and vibrant flowers on food table

Refreshments: Healthy, delicious and beautiful food • Blender "smoothie" drinks • Whole grain baked goodies • Fat-free foods • Fresh fruits and vegetables • Yogurt yummies

Prizes/Favors: Visors • Hats • T-shirts • Exercise books, videos and tapes • Health food items • Vitamins • Natural gifts products

PLAY THE AD GAME

A very commercial theme for the whole family, designed around memorable (groan or grin) ad campaigns from television, radio, or print.

Invitation: Instant copied collage of print ads as mat for the printed invitation • Sent in a manila window envelope trimmed with stickers, rubber stamped messages and hand-written sales slogans [One of the few times that typed labels are suggested...if name is slightly mis-spelled, that'll be even better.]

Dress: To represent a famous advertisement or commercial [move over Brooke!]

Activities: Advertising Trivia game • Creating commercials and videotaping them • Matching "ad to product" game • Souvenir instant photos taken in a famous ad set • Info-mercials presented • Sing along of commercial themes • Name that Tune of ad themes [Uh Huh!]

Refreshments: Heavily advertised products served in their packaging (especially snacks) • Colorful and recognizable boxes, cans and bottles as decor on the buffet table and in the centerpieces • [Coach wait staff to make commercial comments as they serve meal..."You deserve a break today."]

Prizes/Favors: Cents-off coupons • Ad specialty items • Logo products • Antique advertising items

AMERICAN BANDSTAND

This Fifties & Sixties theme is great for transporting nostalgic guests...back in time. The judges are sure to give your party a score of "100," because it had such a great beat.

Invitation: A 45 record with invitation details printed on its label • Or bobby sock with the printed information tucked inside • [Tip: Purchase two socks for each invited guest, but send only one sock per invite. Request that socks be presented to receive matching sock plus a pair for accompanying guest...You can then return any unopened socks.] • Or photo of guest(s) of honor in their bandstand best

Dress: In authentic Philadelphia television dance fashions...date duds or slick-chick styles • As top-forty recording artist or group

Activities: [What else? Dance up a storm, both in and out of the "spotlight"] • Video or audio taped performances of top musical groups of the day to be judged 1--100 by a teen panel • Lip syncing • Karaoke singing • Dance contests • Prizes for Best Costume and Highest Hairdo • Tape and watch

Decor: Bandstand TV studio set • Dick Clark type acting as host • Spotlight dance areas • Giant musical notes • Record album mobiles • TV cameras (prop or real) • Real groovy stuff

Refreshments: Philly sandwiches • Mashed Potatoes • Chicken • Peppermint Twists • Dr. Pepper • Lollipops • Table decorated with 16 Candles

Prizes/Favors: Bandstand collector albums, tapes, videos • Books on the era • Photos of Dick Clark • Gag gifts of giant cans of hair spray decorated with glitter and gold stars to be presented as trophies

BEATLEMANIA

They've got a ticket to fun! Fans of the Fab Four can go bananas donning wacky wigs and Eton Suits straight from Carnaby Street, taking off on those four distinctive personalities. There was "Something" in the way they sang.

Invitation: A poem composed of Beatle song titles that incorporates all information • Printed on light cardboard to replicate record album cover • Guests instructed to call voice mail greeting of poem similar to invitation, ending with a request for R.S.V.P. • Beatle music in background

Activities: Beatle trivia game • Costume contests • Beatle sing alongs • Karaoke performances • Air bands • Arrivals video taped, then tape shown throughout the party for a great laugh-a-minute show

Prizes/Favors: Beatle albums, tapes, photos • Books about one or all • Tickets to concerts, if available • Ed Sullivan Show debut performance video

Refreshments: A variety of English ales • Fish and chips snacks • Traditional English dinner fare

Decor: English Pub atmosphere • Record album covers both on walls and hanging as mobiles • Posters, photos, news articles, movie promo pieces and magazine covers • (All may be obtained from local collectibles outlets, music stores or from mail order companies.)

BEER TASTING PARTY

For the real connoisseur of ale, lager, suds and "brewskis." Fill up the tankards, steins, pilsners or "kegger" plastic cups and get ready for a barrel of fun.

Invitation: Customized invitation printed on a beer can or bottle label. [The more authentic the label is, the bigger the impact.] • Mailed in cardboard carton • Or beer can mailed with invitation tucked inside, with just an outside mailing label • [NOTE: Send a sample to yourself and see if it reaches you.]

Activities: Beer tasting • Beer Barrel Polka'ing • Beer trivia game • Cooking-with-beer recipe demonstrations • For the wild and young ones...beer drinking contests [Wasn't it called Chug-a-Lug?]

Prizes/Favors: Beer mugs • Pilsner glasses • Imported or specialty beers • Beer recipe books • Gift certificates from local beer halls • Hats and t-shirts

Decor: Posters • Beer ads and memorabilia • Beer can garlands and mobiles • Huge inflatable beer bottles and cans • [Pursue your local beer distributors or liquor stores for discarded display items. You may get lucky and run into some real treasures like outdated premium items that can be used as guest gifts and favor goodies.]

Refreshments: Brats • Hot dogs • Hamburgers • Snacks and other beer compatibles • Any recipes such as beer and cheese soup, etc. (See the Garbage Can Dinner Party.)

BLUES IN THE NIGHT

A theme to chase away the blues...by celebrating them. Colorful guests can get creative... until they're blue in the face.

Invitation: Paper and ink any shade of blue • Adorned with ribbons, lace, yarn, feathers glitter and endless trims in many hues of blue

Dress: "Azure" someone or something with the word blue in his/her/its name such as Alice Blue Gown, The Blues Brothers, Blue Beard, etc.

Decor: [Duhhhhhhh! Let me think...Oh, I've got it!] Anything and everything blue! • Buffet table cloth of blueprint paper • Sheet music...of the blues songs...for place mats • Blue bells, blue birds and blue velvet

Activities: Dancing to and singing the blues • Name That Tune with the word "blue" in the title • Art activities such as finger painting limited to a palette of blues, to be presented to the guest of honor • [If your guests can stand it...show the movie, Blue Lagoon] • A challenging game of Blue Trivia with the dramatic presentation of first prize...A BIG BLUE RIBBON!

Prizes/Favors: Blues records and tapes • Bluebird houses • Blue jay prints • Blue jeans

Refreshments: Blueberry pie, muffins, jam and popsicles • Blue Bonnet products • Blue Ribbon Beer • That blue Smurfy juice

7

BREAKFAST AT TIFFANY'S

Brunch for the Veddy Ritzy Bunch. A hoity-toity gathering designed as a social climbing spoof loaded with high-tone laughs.

Invitation: Formal, engraved or specially lettered • Tiny rhinestones glued on the R.S.V.P. period dots • Trimmed with lace, pearls, cords of silver and gold • Sprinkled with sparkle and glitter to dazzle your guests into a festive and fancy RSVP of YES

Dress: Ultra posh • Formal • Dripping with real or fake diamonds and precious gems • Fluffy and faux furs

Activities: Fashion Show of glamorous and glitzy fashions • Prize to the best dressed • Sophisticated violin or harp music • Genteel gossip • Toasts and tributes

Prizes/Favors: "Fabulous Fakes" diamond jewelry • Crystal-like knick knacks • Imitation gold and silver "knock-offs" • Phony designer doo dads • Books, tapes, videos of get-rich-quick schemes • Gag gifts for the person who has everything • Elegantly wrapped next-to-useless gadgets, gimmicks and gizmos • Gift for Guest of Honor: a wonderful silver serving tray with the date and all guests names engraved in a lovely design on the surface.

Decor: Glamor, glitter and glitz • Luxurious lamé and lace • Crystal chandeliers and candelabra • Sparkly and shiny fabrics and papers • Elegant table settings and exclusive decorator touches • [Check with your local department store or community theater for display and prop items that may be rented.]

Refreshments: A beautifully and exquisitely presented brunch with silver, crystal, fresh flowers, linens and lace to richly complement the theme

BROADWAY BASH

Give best regards to guests when they strut their stuff as Broadway Babes, Fair Ladies or Dolls escorted by their Guys.

Invitation: Black and white instant-printed playbill with the evening's events presented as acts of a play...actors' bios describe the host and hostess, guest of honor, along with some fictitious guests...credits include names of attendees • Show ticket design

Dress: As Broadway show characters: Cats to Sugar Babies, Daddy Warbucks to the Phantom • Less theatrical simply dressed up as formal first-nighters or fans

Activities: Rehearsed performances • Broadway Trivia game • Posed on-stage instant photos • Caricatures • Chorus line contests • Karaoke singers belting Broadway show hits • Local theater company troupe to perform • Friend or neighbor to pose as a ticket scalper on your front walk when your guests arrive

Prizes/favors: Tapes, CD's, albums • Books • Posters and promotional souvenirs • Grand, grand prize of either Broadway or local road show tickets

Decor: Show bills • Stage sets, backdrops and props • Lighted sign to welcome guests, giving title and star; e.g., Betty's Broadway Birthday Bash, starring Betty Smith

Refreshments: After theater fare à la Sardi's, The Tavern on the Green or the Carnegie Deli • Dinner served theater style • Intermission bell rung for dinner

BUTTONS & BOWS

I've got a "notion" that they'll like this one. Guaranteed to push all of the guests' funny buttons! A theme that might be so amusing...it'll split their seams.

Invitation: At least one button and one bow glued or sewn to a printed piece • Or printed on "campaign" style pin-back buttons

Dress: As anyone or anything that includes "button" or "bow" in its name • Little "Bow" Peep, Red Buttons, "Bow" Brummel, "Bow" Derek, Clara Bow, Button Gwinnett and more "Bowgus" characters

Activities: On-the-spot photo buttons • Best Costume contests • Sing along to theme songs like "Buttons & Bows," "Tie a Yellow Ribbon," "Button up Your Overcoat" • Old parlor games such as Button, Button—Who's Got the Button? or Pin the Bow on the Bow Wow • Demonstration of Bow Making

Prizes/Favors: Gag buttons • Instant bow-makers • Gift wrapping items • Sewing notions • How-to books • Hair bows • Bow ties • Ornamental button covers

Refreshments: Button mushrooms • Pasta bows • "Bow"ls of punch

Decor: Bountiful buttons and bunches of bows • [Button down these decorations and take a "bow."]

10

CLOWNING AROUND

Everybody loves a clown, watching a clown, or being a clown. Closet clowns will get the chance to show their secret identity and become the persona of their most vivid fantasy.

Invitation: A black and white coloring book-like drawing of a clown on the cover • A color crayon or two attached • Information inside

Dress: In clown garb of choice, with or without makeup • Or costumes brought to trade

Activities: Expert to teach and apply clown makeup • Professional clown to coach in acting, magic, juggling, balloon twisting • Clown costume contest • Posing for instant photos presented in colorful frames • Calliope music

Prizes/Favors: Bozo the Clown books • Balloons • Tickets to the circus • Clown posters and photos • Ceramic, knick knack and souvenir clowns

Decor: Circus flyers and advertisements • Popcorn and cotton candy machines • Ticket booths • Big-top canopies • Clown effects such as giant "anything," wigs and hats • Circus memorabilia • Huge popcorn boxes and giant clown shoes as containers • Lots of balloons • [Remember, the circus capitol of the world is in Sarasota, Florida.]

Refreshments: Standard circus, carnival fare served in the official cardboard serving ware

Random · Thoughts ....

....

....

....

....

....

....

COMEDY TONIGHT

Funny Business at its best with lots of laughs for, by, and about the guests as they get the chance to pay tribute to comic characters, comedians and humor. Seriously!

Invitation: The Sunday comics or a comic book as a mat for a printed invitation comprised of one liners [Bring your significant other... please!]

Dress: As a favorite comic strip character, comedian or funny television personality

Activities: Professional stand-up comic to entertain • Guests performing stand-up routines • The latest in Karaoke: stand-up routines for audience joke-along • Videos of popular comedians in performance • Game: some guests have punch lines and others have cartoons taped to their name tags. As guests mingle, they make matches and register for the grand prize drawing • A Comedy Trivia game at each table, awarding prizes to each person at the first table with all answers correct

Prizes/Favors: Tickets to comedy clubs • Humor albums & videos • Joke books and calendars • Punch line t-shirts • Goofy hats • Gag gifts

Decor: The funny papers • Silly posters and photos • One liners "bannered" about • Comedy stage

Refreshments: Favorite party foods, snacks and appetizers • Foods labeled using as many gag lines or puns as you can stand... literally a groaning table • Guests quench their thirst in the Punch Line

COUCH POTATOES

Television viewers extraordinaire get their chance to show off their couch slouching skills. All of the "sofa spuds" can sit and snack.

Invitation: TV Guide cover created with a banner headline announcing the party...details written inside mock-up in the form of television program schedule • A membership application to the National Couch Potato Organization included [there really is one!]

Dress: Pajamas, robes, fluffy slippers and any designated comfortable "couch couture" or "sofa style"

Activities: Non-stop TV-watching • Videos or television programs on sets in every corner • Rowdy games of TV Trivia, Jeopardy, Wheel of

Fortune • "What program to watch" arguments •
Quick-draw remote control contests • Video and
watch • Battle of the late shows (Dave versus Jay
versus Arsenio versus etc.)

Refreshments: All types of potatoes...and
lots of them • Served and eaten hurriedly during
the commercials • Tons of junk food strewn about
the house within arm's length of guests to prevent
anyone having to glance away from the screen •
Map of Idaho as tablecloth • TV dinners on TV
trays

Prizes/favors: T-shirts and hats •
Monogrammed (magic marker will do) couch
potato pillow cases • Television gossip magazine
• TV Guide • Game show games • Batteries for
remotes • Hemorrhoid donuts and other equally
sophisticated boob tube treasures

DOCTOR, LAWYER, INDIAN CHIEF

Here's an "all work" theme that makes a
playful party for celebrating events that have to
do with jobs, employment or even unemployment.
Make short work of this plan.

Invitation: Newspaper want ads used as a
mat, a good-sized section removed (along the

official ad lines) • "Wanted: Guest for Theme Party" ad inserted, stating all party particulars

Dress: As your dream occupation or job description, real, fictional or imaginary • In uniform carrying tools of the trade; i.e., hard hat and tool belt

Activities: Matching photos of famous people to their occupations on answer sheet... those with all correct answers have chance at prize drawings • Game: During the first hour of party all guest conversation must include references to their dream occupation. If caught out of character by another guest he/she loses 100 dollars fake money [unless they are all doctors, lawyers or Indian chiefs, then they can afford to give real money]...winner with most "moolah" takes the prize.

Prizes/favors: "Get Ahead" type books and tapes • A copy of the old top-forty hit "YIP, YIP, YIP, YIP, YIP, etc. Get a Job!" [Or how about a Village People album? They had good jobs.] • Organizational items • To Do List pads • Day planners • Hy and Lois job jars

Refreshments: Lunchroom cafeteria style • Lunch boxes with sandwiches, fruit and dessert and Thermos jugs filled with party beverage (Call ahead to thrift stores to find out how many lunch boxes and Thermos bottles they have in stock and their cost. Spray paint and decorate these beauties.) • Or elaborately decorated and personalized brown lunch bags/boxes full of goodies

Decor: Want ad pages • Job applications • Magazine photos of workers • Work clothes such as hard hats, painter's pants, lumberjack shirts and miscellaneous work equipment • Lunch pails and brief cases to hold snacks • Old timeclock for guests to punch in and out

FAMILY TIES

Try kinfolk reunions...feudin' and fightin' or kissin' kuzzins. These get togethers can be mighty excitin'. Actually, it is a "relatively" good theme for any friendly gathering—for work or play mates or kin.

Invitation: Mock family photo album using a group photo from the 20's or 30's reprinted as the cover...FAMILY ALBUM printed on cover of card with complete details of party on inside

Dress: As a representative of any famous family (real or fictional), renowned brothers or sisters, musical groups, political, television or movie families

Activities: Portraits of your guests in old-fashioned setting placed into souvenir frames • Rousing rounds of the Family Feud game • Family Fact Trivia game with competitions between families • Game: Guests instructed to bring a photo of their parents or children to be posted. Then, instant photos of each arriving guest or couple are posted. Assign a number to each guest photo and a letter to each of the family photos. Winner makes the most matches.

Prizes/Favors: Photo albums • Family tree charts • Books and videos on famous families • How-to genealogy • The Family Feud board game • All-in-the-Family or Family Ties memorabilia

FASHIONS & FADS

Celebrate the outrageous, news-making, controversial or earth changing fads, trends or fashions. This theme will never go out of style.

Invitation: A poem describing the party printed on a "psychedelic color" paper • Mat on geometrically designed paper • Mailed in an envelope with marbleizing for a tie-dyed effect.

Decor: Garments or linens of geometric or tie-dyed fabrics. Cut into strips and squares and used for napkin ties, centerpiece ribbons, name tag trim • Large fabric items such as geometric patterned drapes used as table clothes, back-drops or furniture throws • Anything psychedelic • Lava lamps • Pet rocks • Wild prints • Polyester fashion statements • Velvet paintings [or are they still in???] Crocheted anything • Bead curtains • Bean bag chairs

Dress: In Nehru jackets • Bell bottoms • See-through garments • Fringy vests • Topless/bottomless garments that let it all hang out • "Grunge"

Activities: Hula Hoop contests • Fad dances • "Biggest Fad or Fashion Flop" contest

Prizes/Favors: Items that are back • Wild ties, patterned socks, designer duds • Nostalgia records and tapes • Anything that says "I ♥" something • Collectibles of the future (Coke stuff, Barbie stuff, Ninja Turtles, baseball cards)

Refreshments: Blend fad and fashion foods with favorites, fetishes and fantasies.

FORTUNE FEST

Take a peek into the future with a party featuring all ways of fortune telling. Tomorrow is utterly fascinating when it is revealed today.

Invitation: In a fortune cookie • Or written in horoscope style with stars, moons and predictions • Or only a phone number sent with instruc-

tions to call for an invitation on a voice mail box •
[I predict that if your recorded message forecasts
fun you will get nothing but positive ESP RSVP's.]

Dress: Gypsy • Wizard • Guru or...Mystic

Activities: The reading of tea leaves,
palms, handwriting, tarot cards, numerology,
crystal ball • Ouija boards • Spooky seances •
[For the skeptic...a dart board with fantasy fortunes written upon it.]

Prizes/Favors: Customized fortune cookies
• Games such as "Wheel of Fortune" • Chinese
fortune cards • Crystal balls • Astrological items
such as calendars, charts, books • [One host had
the handwriting of each guest analyzed pre-party
and had the results waiting at each guest's dinner
place.]

Decor: Magical • Occult or mystical posters
• Art and prop items • Many moons and scads of
stars

Refreshments: A variety of favorite party
foods presented on a buffet table that is decorated with gossamer, stars, magic trick props,
crystal balls and tarot cards

Random • Thoughts ....

....

....

....

FUTURE FANTASIES

Step into the future with space age technology and whimsical futuristic inventions. Instruct guests to wear costumes and carry props that predict the lifestyle of the 21st century.

Invitation: State of the art computer graphics and laser art • Holograms or LED items • Or written on mylar paper • Sent in a clear space tube • Or a space kit of Martian "boinger" head gear, hologram glasses and security I.D. badge sent in a pizza box..."Top Secret," "Security," "Classified" and other warnings written on top of box • Voice Mail RSVP: Space Odyssey music and voice distortion on recorded message

Dress: In space age as gadgets and gizmos of tomorrow • Star Trekkie characterizations • Occupations or recreations of the future

Activities: Game: Match descriptions of technological developments with their actual names. Mix in several phony descriptions and names. Guests are challenged to determine the real from the fabricated • Game: Magazine photos or drawings of ultra-new products are tacked to the walls for teams of three to identify. Teams with the most correct answers win cosmic prizes.

Decor: Mylars and modernistic mirrored fabrics • Laser lights • Holograms • Futuristic posters and art • Slide show of space scenes to create a continuous dramatic display

Prizes/Favors: Books • Magazines • Catalogs • Inexpensive items state-of-the-art calibre • Mylar or hologram novelty items

Refreshments: A table that is "out of this world" using the same fabrics and props mentioned in the Decor section • Menu items simulating those served aboard the space shuttles • Labeled foods/beverages to include: Mars bars, Milky Way, Heavenly Hamburgers, Lil' Orbit donuts, Satellite Stew, Constellation Rations, Big Dipper Ice Cream, Solar Cola

GILLIGAN'S ISLAND

Set sail to this television theme which now has a growing cult following. Feature silly survival tactics, treasure hunts and star-search theatrics for the marooned.

Invitation: Rolled up inside a plastic bottle... treasure map, sand, shells, tiny compass, telescope and complete instructions included (Plastic bottles can be mailed "as is" with label and postage attached.) • Voice Mail RSVP: Recorded message with theme song playing in background

Dress: As one of the characters from the television show (either assigned or let guests choose)

Activities: Guests create shelters, decor, food service, and music as part of their entertainment • Ingredients with detailed instructions and supervision prepared for guests • Island dancing • Treasure hunts • Crafty contests • Costume competitions

Prizes/Favors: Sunglasses • Palm fans • Inexpensive sandals ($1.00 per pair) • Sailor hats • Mini-treasure chests filled with goodies

Refreshments: Any and all typical island delicacies, prepared and served in authentic tropical style

Decor: All the island trappings: Palm trees, grass hut, grass skirts, tropical flowers, tiki lights, beautiful island-hopping music to set the scene • Coconuts, shells and fish net to decorate the table

Go For The Gold

Whether they're talking about Gold Medals, Gold Doubloons or Golden Arches this is a 24 Karat theme. The prospects for fun are genuine, especially with the "Midas" touch.

Invitation: All that glitters...goes on that invitation: glitter dust, stars, confetti, ribbon, cord, chains, lace, fabric and paper • Addressed in gold ink • Sent in a see-through plastic envelope

Dress: In Gold, Gold and More Gold • As Goldie Hawn, Goldfinger, Goldilocks Gold Dust Twins, Solid Gold dancer, etc.

Decor: Go-go-gold • Gold records • Pots of Gold • Gold ribbons • Glitter curtains • Gold Lamé • Goldenrod • Chains, chunks and nuggets • Table linens, serving dishes—gold decor galore

Activities: Prize winner games such as Goldfish Bowl Game • Panning for Gold • Gold Coins in the Fountain • Name that Tune...all the gold songs

Refreshments: á la "Golden Arches" • Golden Plump Chicken • Goldfish snacks • Items that are gold in color including squash, corn bread, a pot of honey and golden ear corn

GO FLY A KITE

Wish for a great day, gather at an open field, and provide kites for all guests. In case of rain plan some spirited and creative kite "making for the taking" and for use on the next high flying day.

Invitation: Small kites made of tissue and popsicle sticks • Or kid's kindergarten-style drawing of a kite with a real string of tails attached • Sent rolled up in tube

Dress: In casual, loose and comfortable "kite flying clothes" • Fleet-of-foot footwear to help runners keep up with those billowing kites

Activities: Horseshoes • Badminton • Variety races • Flying kites, kites, kites

Prizes/Favors: [See if this flies—anything to do with kites] • Unique kite varieties • Books about kite making • Gimmick/gift kite items

Refreshments: Potluck, picnic fare... served on the ground on spread out blankets • Thirst quenching beverages

HAPPY BIRTHDAY
TO EVERYONE

Super gala birthday party to joyfully celebrate all guests' birthdays. Each guest brings a cleverly gift-wrapped generic adult toy to be exchanged

Invitation: Old fashioned fill-in-the-blanks birthday invite, kids style preferred...complete instructions on separate sheet • Or imprinted on balloon • Or complete party kit: party hat, hornblower, streamer and goodie bag sent with instructions in a pizza box

Dress: In best party clothes, children's chic couture

Decor: Balloons • Streamers • Gala party decorations

Activities: Typical party games: Pin the Tail, Musical Chairs, Blindman's Bluff • Clowns making balloon sculptures and painting faces • Photo sessions • An elaborate process of exchanging gifts • Community "Happy Birthday" sung gathered around cake and blowing out many, many candles

Refreshments: Enormous birthday cake with each guest's name iced on it or written on a tiny toothpick flag • Ice cream, soda pop, mint candies and nuts

Prizes/Favors: Party hats and paper blowers plus a colorful goodie bag filled with candy, gifts, and fabulous freebies for all Birthday Kids.

Random · Thoughts ....

....

....

....

HATS OFF TO...

Just off the top of my head, this is a capper of a theme. A very special way to let someone know that he/she is absolutely tops in everyone's hearts.

Invitation: Information written on or tucked inside party hat • Or on standard white folding hat (worn by restaurant employees) decorated with feathers, sequins, glitter, ribbons, stickers

Dress: Wearing favorite hat to match a costume • Or wearing all black clothing to put focus on extraordinary hat

Decor: Hats, caps, chapeaus, berets, bonnets, derbies, tams, or sombreros as center-pieces and as serving containers on the buffet table • Tiny novelty hats as place cards or name tags • Mobiles made of drawings or photos of hats • Antique hat boxes filled with snacks, flowers or favors

Activities: On-the-spot Trim-a-Hat contest • Best original hat contest...prize to the "baddest hatter" • Instant photos of each hat-wearing guest or couple for a take-it-home favor • [Don't forget to do the Mexican Hat Dance!]

Prizes/Favors: Hat shop gift certificates • Sports hats and visors • Hat-related gift items

INTERNATIONAL FOOD BAZAAR

Each guest (or couple) is instructed to bring a special dish representative of their own or favorite ethnic background. They'll be asked to share any tradition associated with their recipe.

Invitation: Recipe card trimmed with flags • Or map • Or travel folder • Or food items such as pasta, bread sticks or fortune cookies mailed with instructions in pizza box or small carton

Dress: In costume of recipe's ethnic origin or dressed as a chef wearing national colors

Activities: Food demonstrations • Ethnic music and dance • Friendly, free-for-all sampling of all dishes • Voting for "bests" • Awarding prizes

Prizes/Favors: Cookbooks • Recipe Organizers • Foreign travel books • Ethnic music on record or tape • Grand and great gourmet items for prizes • A booklet collection of all recipes featured at party presented to each guest as a take-home gift

Decor: 'Round the world food stations • Flags from every nation represented

:24:

INVENTIONS & INNOVATIONS

A tribute to inventions or innovations that have changed our lives. Highly imaginative guests will love this chance to wear concocted costumes and get-ups of their own invention.

Invitation: Magazine ads of ultra modern products or innovations provide mat for your printed piece • Or tiny wire, coils, odd pieces of light weight computer or electrical supplies to create an experimental effect mailed in a plastic see-through tube

Dress: As mad inventors, scientists, craftsmen or as an invention itself

Activities: Invention Trivia game • Guess the Gadget game • Mini-demonstrations of all-new concepts or cutting edge products

Refreshments: Incredible invention edibles: Several food-preparation appliances lined up for a hilarious buffet; i.e., waffle iron, Fry Baby, donut maker, Hotdogger (TV info-mercial type products are perfect.)

Decor: Posters, sales aids • Replicas of inventions • Giant light bulbs • Wires and lights

Prizes/Favors: Gizmos, gadgets and gimmicks!...guests get to grab!

KINDERGARTEN KRAZIES

Kids' play for grown-ups. Create a colorful play school arts and crafts area. If event is planned for outdoors, a beautiful picnic/play area with a full playground will make it a perfect outing.

Invitation: Kindergartners' art work of construction paper, color crayons, string, peppermint paste • Created by the class of a local preschool • All entrants awarded a prize • Addresses written by upper class grade-schoolers

Dress: In t-Shirts, shorts & sneakers • Favorite kids' gear: Disney, Barney, Ninja Turtles • For authenticity—OshKosh by Gosh and Geranimals

Activities: You-name-it kids' games • Creative craft projects • Snack-time • Story time • [Don't forget to take a little nap on your blankie.]

Refreshments: "Help Yourself" peanut butter and jelly, chips, yogurt, popsicles, raisins, fruit and animal crackers • Hot dogs, pizza, hamburgers and other fast food fare • Soda pop, KoolAid or milk

Prizes/Favors: Indoor and outdoor active games • Hats • T-shirts • Toys and books • Kids' toys and prizes (can be taken home or generously donated)

LIBRARY/BOOKWORM BASH

Guests depict a favorite book title, fictional character or author. The literary or "looney" will have a volume of fun with this cultural theme.

Invitation: Bookmark • Or library card • Or mini-book jacket designed with endorsements from guests with facts about the guest of honor incorporated into party information

Decor: Shelves of books (or mural of bookshelves) • Posters • Library memorabilia, such as "quiet" signs • Giant bookmarks • (Check with your local book store for outdated display items.)

Activities: Literary Trivia game • Reading aloud • Matching Book To Author game • Lively game of Charades featuring book titles

Prizes/favors: Dictionaries • Dictionary games • Books • Bookmarks • Magazines • Tickets to author events or signing parties

Refreshments: Recipes prepared from special cookbook [Use those cookbooks as part of the buffet table decor or as centerpieces on the tables.]

27

LITERARY LOVERS

Famous romantic couples portrayed in fiction or non-fiction books will show up. There are dozens of lovers to write home about, starting with Romeo and Juliet.

Invitation: A love poem including all of the pertinent information...neatly handwritten, printed on parchment paper, then tied with a satin ribbon • Sent in colorful mailing tube

Activities: Literary Couples Trivia game • Acting out short playlets • Dancing to romantic music, recorded or live • Love-song sing along • Strolling violinists playing dreamy, romantic dinner music

Decor: Antique volumes amidst whisper-soft tulle, seductive lace and satin • Delicate flowers and greens • Sentimental posters • Candles and twinkle lights and lavish luminaria

Refreshments: Sensual and scrumptious food that one guest can hand-feed to another, like fruit dipped in chocolate • "Nectar of the Gods" from goblets

Prizes/Favors: Books of poetry • Gift certificates for activities for two: plays, concerts or intimate dinners • Romantic items like special oils, scented candles, games just for two

LONG LIVE THE QUEEN (AND KING)

Herald famous royalty from fiction, real life, or movies and television. Some of the most majestic guests will undoubtedly appear as "King Kong," or "Queen Bee."

Invitation: Scroll decreeing royal command to attend • On bejeweled or crested parchment • Sent in gold or silver mailing tube for a regal touch

Activities: Photo session on Throne [yes, that one too...with a royal flush!] • Games: Royal Rummy, Checkers, Chess • Throne Trivia game... ["What English royalty died on the 'Throne'?" for starters] • Crown decorating contest—treasures and trimmings festooned on cardboard crowns • Trumpeters announcing guests • Royal jesters • Special ceremonial crownings of Queen and King for an Hour • [No beheading, please, unless one should mightily deserve it for acting beneath his/her station.]

Decor: Lots of purple, velvet, ermine, dazzling gem encrusted crowns, precious royal jewels, official scepters and shields • Flags and banners of heraldry • Coats of arms

Prizes/Favors: Faux jewels • Gift certificates to "Burger King" or "White Castle" • Tapes of B.B. King, Prince, or Queen • Books by Ellery Queen, Stephen King or Patty Duke

Refreshments: A regal feast of giant turkey legs, luscious fruits, pastries • Tankards of wine, ale and other lip-smacking libations fit for a King and Queen

MAGICAL MOMENTS

Everything appears to be magic. All sorts of tricks, illusions and miracles can be expected when guests are invited to produce their own feat of magic.

Invitation: Written in invisible ink where the message is magically revealed by holding up to the light bulb • Decorated with magical things like sparkling glitter and stars—glued to stay put!

Dress: Guests' choice, from Houdini to The Wizard • [Magicians in tuxedos and capes accompanied by their assistants in black net stockings would be a sure prize winner.]

Decor: Stars, wands, silks, pouf flowers, rabbits in top hats • Old theatrical posters and artist photos • Magicians' props placed on a stage

complete with a shimmery curtain backdrop •
Huge magician's trunk • Fabulous feather flowers
in vases

Activities: Amazing and amusing performances by guests • Topped off with a spectacular
professional magic act to really dazzle and
bewilder

Prizes/favors: Magic Markers • Rabbit's
foot charms • All kinds of "Magic" memorabilia...
[Johnson, that is]

Refreshments: Favorite party menu served
on a special magic prop—a board balanced
across two sawhorses • Snacks served in top
hats • Array of food served on a carpenter's saw

MARILYN, MY MARILYN

A wild theme where everyone, male and
female alike, dresses as Marilyn, yes Marilyn.
The outcome is outrageous, so be prepared—
don't get caught without a video camera!

Invitation: Cover: Marilyn photo (famous
one with skirt flipping in the breeze) with face
replaced with mylar or mirror-like paper • Message on inside of card written as though from
Marilyn herself • A press-on beauty mark included
for each guest as a "costume starter"

Activities: Screen tests of guests reading a short Marilyn script...video taped and played throughout the party • Raucus contest of guests singing "Diamonds are a Girl's Best Friend"

Decor: Marilyn memorabilia • Platinum blond wigs • Glamorous gowns • Film posters • Movie magazine covers • Props • Paste diamonds galore

Refreshments: Everything that starts with "M" such as M & M's, mousse, meat loaf, mashed potatoes, melon, macaroni & cheese, and more • Mineral water, milk, Mimosas, malt liquor, mint juleps, and muscatel

Prizes/Favors: Any of the multitude of items having to do with Marilyn

Random · Thoughts ....

....

....

....

....

....

....

....

HEROES & HEROINES

Real or fictional heroes come down off their pedestals to attend this party. They'll be wearing their super-capes, medals, ribbons and mighty monograms when they turn out to accept their accolades, tributes, and kudos.

Invitation: Ballot for Hero of the Year • Or prestigious award certificates • Or pertinent information tucked inside mini-trophies (possibly engraved)

Dress: As a favorite hero from real life, movies, television or fiction

Activities: Heroes Trivia game • Watching videos of super heroes • Magazine cover-style photos taken of all the brave and admirable guests to keep as proof of the honors bestowed upon them • Caricaturists to sketch the extolled guests for posterity

Decor: Hero cards • Medals • Trophies • Posters • Comic book covers • Newspaper headlines and big boastful banners

Refreshments: [Of course! You must serve Hero sandwiches and "Kamikazes"...drinking them is a sign of bravery]

Prizes/Favors: Serious or silly trophies and award plaques • Colorful t-shirts and hats with "Our Hero" imprinted upon them

:32:

NERDS & ABSURDS

Guests get decked out in their high-water polyesters, plaid three piece pant suits and frumpy dresses. They slick down their hair, slip into their horn-rimmed glasses, and get craazee!

Invitation: Sent inside a plastic pocket protector that has been personalized with guest's name

Decor: Tacky, wacky and tasteless • Tables draped with fabrics of clashing colors and garish prints • Garage-sale vases filled with dreadful plastic flowers • Prominently displayed white elephant eyesores from the attic and closet— [Now's your chance to use those "priceless" wedding gifts!]

Activities: "Gifts from you-know-where" brought by guests to be used in an exchange where everybody loses [For fund raiser, guests have to pay to get rid of their absurd objets d'art.]

Refreshments: Special menu of down-to-earth tacky food in mismatched dishes • Wildly un-classy linens or paper ware "borrowed" from fast food restaurants add a low-brow touch • White Castle "gut bombs" or "sliders," grandiosely presented on brand new garbage can lids

Prizes/Favors: All tasteless decorations and doggy bags filled with leftovers as awards to "Nerdiest and absurdest" guests

NEW YORK! NEW YORK!

All stops out for this East Coast extravaganza-turned-fantasy-trip. They'll want to be a part of it—the Big Apple.

Invitation: New York Times headline tops off printed invitation...mailed newspaper style—rolled and folded • Or hand delivered for late-breaking news-making impact

Dress: As characters from: Broadway, Greenwich Village, Central Park • [Count on a bag person or two complete with shopping carts.]

Decor: Scenes and sets to surround all of the above dress styles • Ongoing slide presentation of typical NY shots for a great background atmosphere

Refreshments: Coney Islands, deli foods, ethnic foods, pretzels, roasted chestnuts • Variety of big city beverages served à la sidewalk vendor style on carts or tables • More elegant fare delivered to sidewalk tables

Activities: Street and ballroom dancing • Face painters and caricaturists • "Touristy" souvenir photos • At least one slight-of-hand con artist • Horse and carriage rides for outdoor events • Recorded or live performances of show tunes, cool jazz, society or big band music accented by street entertainers—working for tips

Prizes/Favors: Souvenir postcards • Imprinted t-shirts • "Apple," "I ❤" stuff [For a really big fund raising bash, offer a drawing prize of a trip to New York.]

Random · Thoughts ....

....

....

....

....

....

....

....

NIGHT COURT

Retired Judge Harry Stone's crazy collection of nocturnal court kooks, featuring the zany defendants, turn out for late sessions. Guests imitate this motley crew of night crawlers.

Invitation: Fake summons announcing request for guest's appearance in court • Or details written in loquacious legalese including such terms as "beyond a reasonable doubt," "by reason of insanity," "contempt of court"

Decor: Mock courtroom and jail cell setting • Table decor to include black and white stripes, yellow legal pad sheets, gavels of various sizes and Lady Justice and her scales • Wanted posters picturing the guest(s) of honor as the fugitive

Activities: Criminals sent to jail and to gain freedom must pay with a song, dance, trick [or money if for fund raiser] • A rousing sing along to crime/jail songs such as: "Release Me," "JailHouse Rock," "I Walk the Line," "Prisoner of Love," "Tie a Yellow Ribbon," etc.

Prizes/Favors: Instant photo of guest behind bars made into a real "mug"...shot • Books and videos

Refreshments: Great food cafeteria style • Legal libations • Tin plates, cups and utensils • Plastic handcuffs used as napkin holders. [Allow guests one phone call—to call and order a pizza.]

NON-PARTY PARTY

This is a super last minute, come-as-you-are type party that is filled with laughs, creativity and incredible variety.

Here's the plan—guests arrive to find absolutely no trace of a party. Five teams are established. Each team selects, through a random drawing, one of the following categories: decorations, entertainment, party favors, beverages, appetizers. Then, by the same method, each team selects one of the following themes: Italian, Mexican, Chinese, All American or Luau. Teams do not reveal either the category or the theme they have drawn. [Are you still with me?]

Given a limited budget and time frame, teams rush out to make their purchases. The first team back wins a prize. This "non-party" could end up with Italian decorations, Mexican entertainment, Chinese party favors, All American appetizers and Luau beverages. Plus, the meal served by the host would also follow one of the five themes.

Invitation: Very unexciting, just a plain piece of white paper • Information typed in center with lots of white space around it—just the bare facts with no mention of the word "party" • No clues other than the dress code, which is "casual"

Prizes/Favors: Blank books • Blank cassette tapes • Ordinary, uncomplicated, and simple gift items

PARTNERS IN CRIME

Famous criminal couples of either real or fictional infamy put their minds together to pull off the perfect crime. No holds barred...or is it bars hold no one?

Dress: As Mobsters and Molls, Burglars and Bimbos [dressed to hurt but not to kill]

Invitation: 8½ x 11 "wanted" posters, photo replaced with mirror-like paper...fugitive's "vital statistics" to be listed as perfect guest qualities • [F.B.I. could stand for **F**.unny **B**.irthday **I**.nvitation]

Activities: Crime/criminal Trivia game • Instant souvenir photos of each couple against backdrop of jail cell or behind Victorian stocks photo board • "Wanted" poster photo mat • A staged raid with arrests and all • Couples handcuffed together for short intervals only [At fund raisers couples would pay to be independent of each other.] • "Sing Sing" along

Decor: Giant "Wanted" posters • Real or cardboard weapons • Black and white striped garments • Law enforcement badges • Giant fingerprints • Blowups of crime scene photos • Collection of burglary tools as centerpiece

Refreshments: First course: bread on a tin plate and water in a tin cup • Cake decorated with nail files • [Food and beverage so great they'll eat as though it were their last meal!]

Prizes/Favors: Crime and mystery novels • Movie tickets • Videos of "Dragnet," "Hill Street Blues" • Tapes of old radio shows; i.e., "The Shadow," "Sam Spade," "The FBI"

:37:

PIZZA AND PASTA PARTY

Carbohydrate heaven! The hosts provide the pasta and pizza crust. The guests bring the toppings and trimmings to create their own starchy sensations. Atsa' real party!

Invitation: Written on a paper chef's hat • Or a plastic bib • Or a printed piece wrapped around a few pieces of pasta or a bread stick • Mailed in tube or small pizza box

Dress: In any combination of red, green and white so that guests provide a major part of the decor • Chef's outfits

Decor: Italian flags and banners • White tablecloths • Red and green napkins • Bread sticks in centerpieces • Travel and product posters • Candles in wine bottles

Activities: Guests creating meals to suit their tastes • Authentic Italian music • Folk dance lessons • Food preparation demo • [For fund raiser, invite local Chef "Louigi" to come and flip pizza crusts and/or autograph recipe books to be sold for charity.]

Prizes/Favors: Pizza/pasta recipe books • Gift certificates to local pizza/pasta restaurants • Fresh pasta made with your new Popiel Pasta maker...as featured on TV. [The pasta maker could also be a phenomenal raffle prize.]

Random • Thoughts ....

....

....

....

....

....

....

POLKA FEST

They'll kick up their heels to an "oom-pah" polka band and dance off the beer, brats and potato salad. An ideal fall festival event...if anyone's Polish, so much the better.

Invitation: A cassette of a spoken invitation recorded with lively polka music in the background...colorful custom label on tape...mailed with printed invitation in padded envelope

Dress: In authentic or contrived costumes of brightly colored shorts, skirts, vests and shawls

Decor: National flags • Folk costumes • Colorful travel posters • International maps • Beer barrels

Activities: Polka instructions • Entertainment by folk dancers • Best costume contests • Costumed guests posing for instant photos

Refreshments: Brats, potato salad, sauerkraut, spaetzel, strudel and noodles • Beer from the barrel

Prizes/Favors: [Who wouldn't want to win a copy of Bobby Vinton's famous Polish Anthem? Second prize?... two copies!] • Beer mugs, steins and fancy pilsner glasses • Specialty beers or wines • Cookbooks and ethnic food products

LIFESTYLES OF THE RICH AND FAMOUS

Robin Leach or not, go ahead and have a ball (fancy, of course) with this dramatic and theatrical theme—rich with fun.

Invitation: Elegant, formal, engraved look, beautifully addressed • Mailed or presented in person • Use of upscale words such as "Jet Set," "villa," "abroad," and "yacht" • Voice Mail RSVP: Recorded message of Robin Leach sound-alike

Dress: In furs, jewels, finery of the utmost in superficial taste • Black tie or better • (Over-dressing strongly encouraged.)

Activities: Sing along replaced with boast along...each guest giving a short summary of his/her latest purchases of expensive belongings • Any silly spoof on the very, very rich • Demonstrations: diamond polishing, cooking with Caviar Helper • Dancing to so very swanky society music (if recorded, display large mural of orchestra) • Uniformed butler formally announcing guests as they arrive

Decor: Crystal chandeliers • Candelabra • Elegant fabrics • Ultra-elaborate floral arrangements • Anything ostentatious or pretentious

Refreshments: Butlers and maids serving fake or real champagne in fake or real crystal; fake or real paté on fake or real silver platters • Exotic menu and lavish decor

Prizes/Favors: Fancy shopping bag imprinted with: "For the person who obviously has everything, a status bag to carry it in." • Instant photos of the nouveau riche guests affixed attractively to their bag to personalize it

SIT-COM SOCIAL

The TV shows: Family Ties, Married With Children, MASH, Cheers are all rich with characters who will come out of syndication for a super costume party.

Invitation: TV Guide cover with honored guest's picture on it • Information printed inside • Guests RSVP with the day and hour that their selected character appears on TV

Dress: As Hawkeye and Trapper • Sam, Norm and Cliff • Roseanne and Dan • Murphy • Blossom • Al and Meg...etc.

Decor: Recognizable sets from popular sit-coms

Activities: Sit-Com Trivia-thon • Videos of sit-com re-runs • Costume contests • Name that Tune for sit-com theme songs • A rousing theme song sing along. • Video and watch

Refreshments: "Mash"-ed potatoes • Buffalo "Wings" • "Roseanne" Bars, etc. • TV Dinner trays for serving

Prizes/Favors: Videos • Customized t-shirts • TV fact books • Mugs • Instant photo buttons

ST. VALENTINE'S DAY MASSACRE

The famous 1920's slaughter inspires folks to plan gangster parties all year round. Flappers and dappers kick up their heels, hoping the Feds won't show up and stop the music, which would prohibit their frolic.

Invitation: An offer they can't refuse— Printed invitation telling guests to watch the local personals for an important password...a must-have for getting in to the party...trimmed with white lace, blood red hearts • Or pretend pearls and red satin ribbon bow ties as "costume starter" incentive...sent in padded envelope

Dress: In Roaring Twenties finery, fringy and flirty • Gents in tuxedos or pin striped suits

Decor: Speak-easy peep hole at front door • Intimate nightclub atmosphere • White table-cloths, candles • Small dance floor • Tiny stage and bandstand • Gun check at the door

Activities: Charleston contests • Best costume awards • Dancing to the jazz band • Staged midnight raid by Elliott Ness and his prohibition agents

Refreshments: Drinks served in coffee cups • Bathtub gin • Late night buffet

Prizes/Favors: Goldfish in bowls • While-you-wait photos in art deco frames

STAR SEARCH/ KARAOKE PARTY

It's the rage of the country...sing along Karaoke parties where one can be a star, a contest judge, a talent scout or part of the audience. Once they start singing—there's no stoppin' 'em.

Invitation: Audition announcement, sprinkled with tiny stars (glued, of course) • Or plastic microphones, sprayed silver • (Send a song list sent so that guests can make a selection to rehearse for their debut.)

Dress: As artist known for performance of song selected • Guest judges, talent scouts or emcees

Decor: Mini stage with glitter curtain, spot lights, banner • Karaoke set-up (can be rented in most towns) • Musical instruments • Concert posters • Sheet music

Prizes/Favors: Video or cassette recordings of guests' performances • Star-shaped items such as pillows, paper weights, picture frames, key chains, and so much more • Sing along background tapes • Song books • T-shirts or hats with star motif

Refreshments: Star catering wagon with food for the hungry artists • Backstage buffet with after the concert menu

SUPER SLEUTHS

This one's a tribute to all famous detectives, cops or mystery solvers from books, movies, television or the nostalgic radio era.

Invitation: A tiny magnifying glass attached to sheet of written clues clearly directing guests to party • Sent in black envelope addressed in silver for an intriguing look

Dress: As a famous Who-dunnit character: Charlie Chan, Dick Tracy, Agatha Christie, Sherlock Holmes ["Only the Shadow Knows" how many others.]

Activities: Mystery game with clues that guests must gather from each other, then assimilate for the solution • Mystery Trivia game

Prizes/Favors: Notebook and pencil for gathering clues • Collectibles: Nancy Drew/Hardy Boys novels • Movie mystery videos • Clue game • Where in the World is ...? or other computer games

Refreshments: Named after famous sleuths: Columbo's Combo, Sherlock's Shrimp, Ellery's Celery, Matlock's Meat Loaf, Mrs. Fletcher's Flambé, The Commish's Knishes • Perry's Perrier, Pink Panther Punch, Mike Hammer's Rusty Nails

Random • Thoughts ....

....

....

....

....

....

....

SWISS SOIREÉ

For those fond of fondue, this cook it your-self party theme is ideal! Ski enthusiasts or not— the guests will be at home in an atmosphere reminiscent of a Swiss Alpine chalet.

Invitation: Printed information inside a Swiss Alps travel brochure • Or small piece of Swiss chocolate attached for a tasty and tempting touch • Voice Mail RSVP: Recorded message must include a yodeler!

Refreshments: Brought by guests...an assigned fondue ingredient to serve two (meat, vegetable, fruit) chopped and ready for "dipping" • Provided by host...fondue equipment, cheese, bread and chocolate for dessert dips, wine and/or hot Swiss chocolate

Activities: Ski movies • Fireside sing along • Entertainment by yodelers and Tyrolean musi-cians • Cooking and chatting

Dress: In active or aprés ski clothes or authentic Alpine gear

Prizes/Favors: Anything made in Switzer-land: chocolate, cheese, watches • Recipe books • Fondue equipment • Prize of small bank labeled "Authentic Swiss Bank," a few francs included

Decor: Chalet, lodge or Gasthaus atmosphere • Fireplace (fake or real) • Huge paper snow flakes • Candles and twinkle lights • Travel posters • Ski equipment

45

UNIFORMS UNITE

There's something about a man/woman in uniform...and here's a chance for guests to jump into a dream or fantasy job with the appropriate work apparel.

Invitation: Matted on collage of photos of uniforms • Or embroidered (with paint) badge for each guest sent with printed invitation

Dress: In uniform, either work or military • Musicians in band uniforms • Servers in jackets or vests to represent uniform

Decor: Photos and posters • Uniforms from today or yesterday • Sales brochures from uniform manufacturer or rental company • Swags of typical work fabric; i.e., denims, ticking, grey flannel, etc. • Cover table with khaki, blue or white fabric • Trimmed with gold stars, military stripes • Gold or silver braid used as napkin ties—a very "uniform" table

Refreshments: Mess hall, lunchroom, commissary, company cafeteria, training table fare • Uniform hats to hold bread, snacks, fruit, napkins and eating utensils

Activities: Best Uniform contest • Brass polishing • Routine inspections [Any guest found out of regulation uniform is severely reprimanded.]

WHEEL OF MISFORTUNE

Vanna and Pat, watch out! This party features "the game the whole family plays" as the lead theme, but any game show game can be played.

Invitation: Instant printed sheet spelling out the celebration; i.e., "Sally's Fiftieth Birthday," in Wheel of Fortune style...all letters turned or some missing • Or cardboard wheel with information printed in wheel sections with spinner attached • Sent in computer disc mailer

Dress: In Vanna, Pat or contestant garb

Decor: A studio set, audience seats and a prize display area of new, used, useful or worthless prizes

Activities: Playing the "Wheel" or other game show games • Dancing on a huge "wheel"

painted on the floor • Name Tag game: Tags show just a few letters of the guest's name. Those who correctly guess others' full names receive chips or pennies; guest with the most chips wins prize [but not before he/she solves the final puzzle!]

Refreshments: Money amounts replaced with names of food items on money wheel from casino supplier • Guests spin for dinner [Of course, they all get a complete meal...but not until they are a Spinner Dinner Winner.]

Prizes/Favors: Games, Games and more games

WINNERS AND LOSERS

This party pays tribute to famous winners and losers—real or fictional—from the sports, news, entertainment, business or political arenas.

Invitation: Words "The envelope please..." written on the front of the envelope holding the invitation...secured with official seal, sticker and Academy award style ribbon trim...mailed inside another envelope

Dress: Depicting a winner or loser • Alternatively, formal or down-and-out attire

Decor: Blue first prize ribbons • Huge paper ribbons marked "booby prize" • Giant gold medals • Oversized dunce caps • Campaign posters • Photos of Academy Award winners • Large replica of award statuette designed for event • Table worthy of first prize decorated with ribbons, awards statues, trophies holding flowers, utensils or napkins

Activities: Brief awards ceremony for the best to the worst [Don't forget Blackwell's worst dressed list.] • Gala dinner-dance • Video taped interviews of the recipients of the Winners and Losers Awards played during dessert • A prize for the most original winner and loser concept • Horseshoe arrangement of plastic flowers (as in the Winner's Circle) placed around winner's neck

Prizes/Favors: Trophy designed for the event • Old campaign buttons (losers and winners) • Products that were/are "losers and winners" • Self-help books with "winner" or "loser" in title • Diet books for wanna-be losers • Instant photos of guests wearing horseshoe flowers

Refreshments: Prize winning recipes • All time winners—no losers

Random • Thoughts ....

....

....

SATURDAY NIGHT LIVE

The best of Saturday Night Live's best is rich with characters and scenarios ranging from Mr. Bill to Pat (?) with a "Da Bears" round table thrown in for sports fans.

Invitation: Written instructions to call a voice mail box with pertinent information announced by a President Clinton sound-alike (talent from local comedy club)...sent on mock White House official stationery • Voice Mail RSVP: Recorded message by same phony pres

Activities: Performances of short skits • Watching SNL Videos • Some "Superior" dancing and "Conehead" cavorting • Major SNL Trivia game • Guest music performances on tape

Refreshments: Cheeseburger, Chips! • Tang and Egg Salad • Church Lady's Jello Mold • Other late night treats [They'll like the juice!]

Decor: Blowup photos of SNL favorites • A Wayne's World "Wreck Room" Set • Promo posters for spin-off movies starring alumni: Eddie Murphy, Bill Murray, John Belushi, Gilda Radner, Dana Carvey, Dan Aykroyd, and Chevy Chase

Prizes/favors: SNL stuff • T-shirts and hats • Classic videos • Posters and books from SNL characters

SPORTS HALL OF FAME

Here's something in the "jocular" vein, especially when the guest of honor is a "sportsaholic." This one will be a blow-out victory—and that's no jock!

Invitation: Designed as sports ticket • Or flyer promoting sports event • Or sports program • Or, for the earthy types...a miniature jockstrap or facsimile

Dress: As any sports figure or fanatic fan

Decor: Variety of sports equipment • Posters • Uniforms • Headgear • Magazine covers • Team banners • Signs

Refreshments: Concession stand food such as hot dogs, popcorn, peanuts, CrackerJack • Gatorade (spiked if you like), home team "rootin" root beer, real beer

Activities: "Trivia 'til They Tire" • Sports skill testers such as shooting hoops, power pitching, putt-putt on the green • Some "daring" games of Tiddley Winks for the sedentary • A play-by-play audio tape of a down-to-the wire victory starring the guest of honor—suitable for baseball, football, hockey or basketball

Prizes/Favors: Instant photos—sports magazine cover style • Customized sports cards • Trophies • Sports items galore: apparel, clocks, books, videos, stationery, games

"V" IS FOR VALENTINES

Plan this party so that the name of each component starts with the letter V. Visualize a very viable and vivacious Valentine's Day venue.

Invitation: Printed on vellum • Or on a V-shaped folded card • Trimmed with Valentine hearts • Sent in a variegated envelope • Addressed to V.I.P.'s • Voice mail responses

Dress: In velvet, vests, velour, vintage, Victoria's Secret • As Village People, Valley girls, vampires • From Victorian era

Decor: Voile • Vines • Violets • Vases • Valances • More Velvet • Veils • Voo doo dolls • Voting booths

Refreshments: Variety Vittles, Velveeta, Vienna Sausages, veggies, vichyssoise, vanilla pudding and ice cream • Vino and vodka • Viva towels for napkins • Vending machine on site

Activities: Violinists • Video games • Viennese waltzes • Vocalists • Volleyball • Variety show • Vaudeville acts • Ventriloquists • Vying for valuables • Van rides • Video and Watch

Prizes/Favors: Visors • Volkswagon parts • Volumes • Vitamins • Velamints • Vogue Magazines • Vacuum bags • Velcro • For the big prize—a Vacation • Modified version—Vacation Visions (camera and film)

"H" IS FOR HALLOWEEN

This theme incorporates the same "first letter" concept, except the name of everything planned must begin with the letter H.

Invitation: Handwritten or home made • On a hanky • Or a hologram • Or H-shaped • Or heart shaped • Hand-delivered

Dress: In hip huggers, hula skirts, halos, Hawaiian shirts, high waters, Happi coats, hoods, horn-rimmed glasses, house coats, hoop skirts • As hillbillies, hoboes, hippies, or hockey players

Decor: Half moons • Haystacks • High chairs • Happy faces • Hounds tooth checks • Hawaiian prints • Hammocks • Hassocks • Helium filled balloons

Refreshments: Hamburgers, hash, hickory ham, hot dogs, Hershey bars, hominy grits • Herbal tea, Hawaiian Punch, hot toddies, hot chocolate, H_2O [and how about hootch?]

Activities: Hawaiian dancers • Hoedowns • Harpists • Hog calling • Hula hoops • Hide 'N Go Seek • Hoops • Hay rides • Hockey games • Hip-Hop dancing

Prizes/Favors: Hats 'n horns • How-to books • Hair bows • Hamsters • Hot pads • House plants • Hockey tickets • His 'n hers towels • History books • Handkerchiefs

"N" IS FOR NEW YEAR'S

No, not again! Yes, but this time use things that start with an N. Now or never, nocturnal nuances need night life.

Invitation: Naughty or nice notice or notification • On neon paper or newsprint • Or newsletter form • Or with a nickel or a noodle attached • In a notebook or on a note pad

Dress: Naked [oops!] • In negligees, nylons, night shirts, Nehrus, or neckties • As nurses, newlyweds, Neanderthals, nerds, Ninja turtles

Decor: Netting • Neon lights • Navy blue • Nosegays • Numbers • Nooses • Night lights • Newspapers • Nuggets • Nozzles • Nauticals • Neckerchiefs • Needlework • Nature's Narcissus

Refreshments: Nachos, noodles, nectarines, nuts, nibbles & noshes, napoleons, Nabisco crackers, navel oranges, Neapolitan ice cream • Near beer, nectars, Napa Valley wine

Activities: Nightclub acts • New York songs • Nostalgia music • Newscasts • Nauseating narrations [like this]

Prizes/Favors: Neckties • Nose plugs • Name plates • Novelettes • Nightcaps • Novelties

Random · Thoughts ....

....

....

....

....

....

....

....

....

....

FIRST LETTER OF GUEST OF HONOR'S NAME

This bash features items that begin with the first initial of the Guest of Honor's name. Some initials will lend themselves ideally to this concept, others will not. Fill in the following form with pencil to get an idea if his/her initial could be successfully used.

Invitation: ....

....

Dress: ....

....

Decor: ....

....

Activities: ....

....

Refreshments: ....

....

Prizes/Favors: ....

....

Bonus, Bonus

GARBAGE CAN DINNER PARTY

The meal preparation is a big part of this "Can Luck" party since it is cooked in and served from a new galvanized garbage can. Following are the ingredients needed for one person's meal so that you can multiply them by the number of guests to determine the total amounts needed. You can then determine what each person should bring.

For each person: Two potatoes, two carrots, one half onion, quarter head of cabbage, two brats or polish sausages

For 100 persons: 24 cans of beer

For 50 persons: 12 cans of beer

Instructions:

Start charcoal fire. Surround with rocks to serve as grate.

1st layer. Stand opened cans of beer on the bottom of garbage can.

2nd layer. Cut cabbage in quarters and place on top of beer cans.

3rd layer. Scrub red potatoes and with skins on, place on top of cabbage.

4th layer. Peel and quarter onions, scrub and cut carrots, then place all on top of potatoes.

Place brats or sausages on top of onions and carrots.

Add seasonings: Caraway seeds, salt and pepper.

Place garbage can on top of rocks for about two hours.

When food is ready, remove it layer by layer and spread out on large trays for serving. Drizzle a little melted butter over the vegetables to add a little guilt to this exceptionally healthy meal.

Summary:

- Laying out the charcoals and the rocks for the fire can be done before the guests arrive, but it can also be part of the evening's activities.

- Peeling, cutting, chopping and cooking the vegetables provide a lively and sociable start to the party.

- The steam from the beer and the juices from the vegetables and meat soak and permeate the solids to provide a wonderful hearty meal and a friendly, casual gathering.

BONUS PARTY TIPS

Just a few brainstorms listed in no particular order...some more very • random • thoughts. I hope that you find a few gems to excite or calm you in your theme party "plandemonium."

1. At a sit-down meal event, place a disposable (one-time) camera on each table. Invite the guests to take photos of each other—the more candid and crazy the better. These photos will capture memorable scenes— scenes that you would have missed.

2. An imaginative theme for a holiday open house: A "Dress Up From the Waist Up" party. Invite guests to wear their formal glitter and glitz from the waist up. For the ladies: beaded tops, rhinestone jewelry, boa feath- ers, even cubic zirconia tiaras. For the gentlemen: tuxedo shirts and jackets, fancy ties, top hats. But allow them to "Dress Down" below the waist with Bermuda shorts, sweat pants, sneakers, sweat socks. This versatile theme is perfect for parties that take place in "cozy" quarters—where guests may be required to sit on the floor, steps, etc.

3. Hand-deliver any invitation that comes with perishable or bulky items such as food, flowers, balloons, apparel or gifts. Your messenger must be dressed to fit the theme.

4. Send your guests home with see-through take-home containers filled with surplus food. This is especially practical for fruits, vegetables, dips, cheese, sweets and cake. Festively decorate these goodie boxes with a bow, sticker or "bon appetit" message.

5. Theme party hosts will be thrilled to receive their party invitation either framed or encased in a lucite box. Remember to put a label on the back noting the occasion, date, and your name.

6. A tickler mailing generates excitement and enthusiasm for gala events. Send a postcard or note to invited guests, with or without gimmick attached, one week before the event as a genial reminder that you are looking forward to their attendance. Example: for an Italian Feast send a small packet of parmesan cheese attached to a note that reads "It will be Grate to see you."

7. Select your party site to support your theme. For instance, hoedown in a barn, safari at a zoo, luau at a beach, picnic in a park, tea party in a garden, mystery at a mansion. You will avoid the cost of creating a special atmosphere.

8. Buffet service is currently in vogue. To take off on the salad bar concept here's some help-yourself ideas: Potato Bar, Pasta Bar, Fondue Bar, Crepes Bar, Peanut Butter Bar, Pancake or Waffle Bar, Burger & Brat Bar, Taco Bar, Dagwood Sandwich Bar

CATALOGS FOR THEME PARTY SUPPLIES

ORIENTAL TRADING, Cute stuff for great party favors, decorations and low priced gifts. Huge selection of "mini" items that are perfect for invitations, name tags and place cards. Much, much more at wholesale prices. 800/228-0122

CRAFT KING Discount Craft Supply Catalog, P.O. Box 90637, Lakeland, FL 33804. Anything and everything that you would need to create your own festive and elegant party decor, gifts and promotional items. A great selection of ribbons, lace, jewels, and other crafty items. Send $2.00

SHERMAN PARTY LINE DIVISION, THEME PARTY NOVELTIES CATALOG, for party favors, hats, especially Karaoke Party Props. 800/645-6513, Ext. 3025, Leslie

BENCO PARTY FAVORS CATALOG, another good selection of party items. May have minimums. 800/874-7970

PAPER DIRECT, top-of-the-line paper products for invitations, programs, stationery. Magnificent 4-color art work, ready for copy machine or laser printer. 800/272-7377

ANDERSON'S SPECIAL EVENT DECOR AND FAVORS, has several catalogs for parties, weddings, promotions. 800/328-9640

HULABALOO COSTUME CATALOG, garments and accessories for parties and promotions. 800/726-1970

VIKING OFFICE PRODUCTS, PAPER SALE CATALOG, specialty copy papers, four-color blanks, labels, etc. Great for invitations, programs and promotional materials. 800/421-1222 and ask for location nearest you.

STUMPS PARTY SUPPLIES & DECORATIONS CATALOG, display and theme prop items. 800/348-5084

1993 WILTON YEARBOOK OF CAKE DECORATING, 192 pages brimming with fabulous ideas for creating cakes, candies and "lovin' spoons full" for every special occasion—especially themes. $5.99 in your department store or craft shop or call 708/963-7100 for charge orders

THINK BIG features huge replicas of everyday items such as pencils, crayons, scissors, gavels, and sneakers to make a big impression on your party guests. 800/487-4244

SALLY DISTRIBUTORS, another colorful collection of gifts, party decor, favors and costumes. 800/472-5597

IDEA ART, truly has the most complete collection of special papers for laser printer or copy machine. You will find a paper that is perfect for almost every theme that I have outlined in this book. Paper and envelope for an invitation would cost approximately, 45-65 cents (25 or 100 quantity). 800/433-2278

GIFTS AND PRODUCTS

SWAN PUBLISHING, the source of a "steamy" novel that incorporates the names of your special people into its story. Perfect gifts for engagements, weddings, anniversaries, birthdays or holidays. Information and order sheet 800/535-SWAN

SUPERGRAMS, paper and laminated banners that both decorate and congratulate in a giant way. Speedy turn around delivery accommodates even the most last minute orders. Great prices, too. Request brochure: 800/3BANNER, ask for Doug

PLATABLES, the sensational buffet plates that are designed to hold a beverage container, napkin, utensils and even a toothpick are the perfect solution for those standing room only affairs. May be custom imprinted for a great giveaway item. Request color brochure: 800/833-0696

BIG LEAGUE CARDS, baseball or whatever-sport cards customized with your GOH's picture and information. Ideal favor or announcement. Brochure: 201-692-8228

ADVANCED GRAPHICS, life-size standup cutouts of celebrities for those great instant photo shoots. Large selection from Marilyn to Michael and Presley to the Pres. Call for brochure: 510/432-2262

MASKPARADE, sensational life-size masks created from a copy of the subject's face, adorned and bedecked with special decorative items. They are unforgettable when held up to surprise the guest of honor, and delightful as an invitation or program. Each is a work of art...to put a new face on your party decor. Write for information: 7817-67th Avenue North, Brooklyn Park, MN 55428

KARAOKE EXPRESS, home/work unit is ideal for theme party entertainment. Package includes equipment, 300 songs on CD, two microphones, song list books, and carrying case. Own it for your personal use or share it with fellow members or employees. Call Dan Desmond: 612/644-3609

SONGSENDSATIONS, ultra-custom songs for the person(s) who deserves everything—even his/her/their own song. Dozens of details set to music and recorded on cassette. Includes framed song sheet. Brochure/order form: 73729 Manzanita Court, Palm Desert, CA 92260

PLAY IT BY EAR, a CD Trivia Game that will keep your guests guessing with sounds of sports, news, music, history, nature or literature. Around $40. Available at most Musicland stores

REMINISCING, another trivia game for persons over thirty, teaming up for lively party "brainteasing." Sells for $19.95. Available at department stores or through Colorful Images catalog: 800/458-7999

ELSIE'S CLOSET, vintage fashions for theme parties. She's in Minneapolis but she sells clothes, hats, shoes, etc. mail order to party goers and theatrical folk all over the country. Just ask Disney and Broadway! Give her a call with your specific needs; she'll send a photo for your consideration. Elsie Iverson, 612/825-5627

OUTRAGEOUS FORTUNES, fortune cookies with your message inside. Great as invitations, announcements, favors—they even have one for a lottery. Write for information: Dept. PS, 326 Cedar Avenue South, Minneapolis, MN 55454

PUBLICATIONS FOR PLANNING THEME PARTIES

THE ADDRESS BOOK: HOW TO REACH ANYONE WHO IS ANYONE, by Michael Levine. Great when you want to request auction items or letters of congratulations from celebrities in entertainment, sports, literary, business or political arenas. $9.95 from Perigee Books. Surely at your library and bookstore.

ADDRESSING FOR SUCCESS, a 10 page booklet that has been produced by the United States Postal Service to help business people with their mailings. It will guide you in mailing invitations in envelopes, cartons, tubes or unusual containers. It gives tips that will help you speed your mail along, utilizing their new scanning systems. Ask at your post office Business Mail department.

FOOD FOR FIFTY, nifty recipe book for preparing big batches for big bashes. Published by Shugart-McMillan and available at B. Dalton. Try your library first, though...because it's Food For Fifty for Fifty...[bucks, that is!]

FAMILY REUNIONS AND CLAN GATHERINGS, by Shari Fiock, a public relations pro. Filled with forms, charts, illustrations and a very comprehensive bibliography. You'll really be successful with events planned for "any group united by a common interest or pursuit." Try a library, bookstore or call: 916/842-5788.

BAR/BAT MITZVAH SURVIVAL GUIDE, by Carol Publishing Group. A very complete how-to guide for planners ranging from the novice to the pro. Ideas and trends to keep you current. Library or call 201/866-0490 for name of bookstore nearest you.

The following books will be valuable to you in planning theme wedding or anniversary celebrations. They are all available from Brighton Publications, 800/536-BOOK. Call for color brochure.

WEDDING PLANS: 50 UNIQUE THEMES FOR THE WEDDING OF YOUR DREAMS, by Sharon Dlugosch. A whimsical or traditional, glamorous or low key, sentimental or upbeat plan? You'll be inspired with this 192 page guide. $10.95.

WEDDING OCCASIONS, by Cynthia Lueck Sowden. 101 themes for wedding showers, rehearsal dinners, engagement parties and more. 158 pages, $9.95.

AN ANNIVERSARY TO REMEMBER, by Cynthia Lueck Sowden. Themes to celebrate the first or the fiftieth...actually as high as the seventy-fifth. Sentimental, gala, and for sure, memorable. 159 pages, $9.95.

Random · Thoughts · of · Your · Own

....

....

....

....

....

....

....

....

....

....

....

....

....

....

....

PATTY SACHS LOVES TO HELP YOU!

- If you are stumped for a theme idea or resource I will be happy to try to help you. Just call me and we can chat for a few minutes. We might come up with a solution in no time. There is no charge to you other than the long-distance.

- I also do ½ hour phone consultations that include a typed summary of our discussion complete with ideas and resources. The charge for this is $30.00 and long-distance.

- Our service, **CELEBRATION CREATIONS**, designs and creates wonderful custom theme invitations, name tags, place cards, favors and decorations—all carefully coordinated to enhance your party. We can provide you with the design, instructions and resources for your own do-it-yourself projects. Just call or fax your needs and we will come up with a proposal.

- For a complete party plan that will free you up from the research and development and leave you with the fun, why not give me a call? After we establish your needs, I will give you a proposal.

- For corporation or organization events, you might need an in-person consultation. I will meet with you in your office to assist you in producing a creative and successful party or promotion. Fee and expenses are negotiable.

- **SONGSENDSATIONS**, another of our services, creates the voice mail messages that are so fabulous for your theme party RSVP's. Scripted voice over and music are recorded on your voice mail for $50.00.

- For just a few minutes or for a few days, I love to help plan parties and I'd be pleased to hear from you. Until then, I hope that your life is full of reasons to celebrate.

PATTY SACHS

CELEBRATION CREATIONS

73729 MANZANITA COURT

PALM DESERT, CA 92260

FAX OR PHONE: 619/341-2066

CELEBRATION CREATIONS
Publication Order Form

Newsletters:

___ *Stress-Free Wedding Planning* .... $ 3.00
One-time tip sheet, budget-minded ideas

___ *Stress-Free Planning of Business Events* 20.00
Quarterly newsletter for planners of company parties,
meetings, picnics, open houses and promotions

Books:

___ *Weddings, Parties & Celebrations* $14.95
300 pages, plans, ideas and resources for all
celebrations

Reprints:

(Originally written for seminars, workshops, special
informational sessions or publication.)

___ *How To Plan an Event to Remember* .... $ 4.00
___ *Planning Company Parties and Picnics* 4.00
___ *Twenty P.R. Ideas for Small or
Home-Based Business* 4.00
___ *Rave Review Open Houses* 4.00
___ *Getting Started As a Party Planner* 4.00

Total for newsletters, books and reprints .... _____

(All orders include shipping and handling,
but MN residents must add 6½% sales tax) .... _____

TOTAL ORDER .... _____

Please carry this total to the reverse side and
complete the mailing address and payment information →

TOTAL AMOUNT
carried forward fro

☐ Enclosed is check/money order
    payable to: Celebration Creations
☐ Add my name to your mailing list for notice of
    future publications

Mail order w/ payment to:

CELEBRATION CREATIONS
7817 - 67th Avenue North
Minneapolis, MN 55428

Your Name _____

Title/Company _____

Street Address _____

City/State/Zip _____

Phone (____) _____

Date Mailed _____

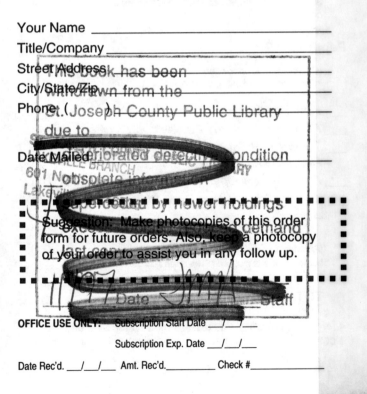

Suggestion: Make photocopies of this order
form for future orders. Also, keep a photocopy
of your order to assist you in any follow up.

_____ Date _____ Staff

OFFICE USE ONLY: Subscription Start Date ___/___/___

Subscription Exp. Date ___/___/___

Date Rec'd. ___/___/___ Amt. Rec'd. _____ Check # _____